COLOR & CRAFT
TEACHER'S APPLE

Pretty Mandala Apple Designs on Keepsake Paper Crafts to Color

EASY PRE-PRINTED PAPER CRAFTS TO COLOR, CUT, GLUE AND MAKE
The Anni Arts coloring crafts are ready to color and craft in this book format.
'Print-on-demand' makes printing as environmentally friendly as printing the crafts at home.

KEEPSAKE PROJECTS TO COLOR AND MAKE:
ART TO FRAME
CARDS AND DECORATIONS
EQUIPMENT GUIDE AND TIPS

GREETING CARDS
5" x 7" and 4" x 6" card toppers to color for art cards or to frame as reusable décor.
MUG CARDS AND TEABAGS: – *Cut into shaped postcards, rectangles or layer the shapes on card.*
TEACUP CARDS AND TEABAGS: – *Cut into shaped postcards, rectangles or layer the shapes on card.*
CUPCAKE CARD: – *Cut into a shaped postcard, rectangle or layer the shape on card.*
Download free blank templates to print as card bases at Anni Arts *https://www.anniarts.com/teacher-clip-art.html*

DÉCOR
LARGE APPLE MANDALA PICTURES: – *To lavishly color and frame*
FESTIVE BUNTING/FLAGS/PENNANTS: – *To color and use as keepsake décor on a wall or over a door or window. Store the bunting in a large envelope to protect them for many years of classroom displays.*
3D APPLE DECORATIONS: – *Pretty items to use for many years. They can be combined with the bunting too.*
CHRISTMAS OR BIRTHDAY STOCKING: – *Use it as a gift packet for candy, money or a gift card.*
TAGS: – *Double-layered to get the thickness for tags. Glue and cut when dry. Punch a hole for the tag.*
LABELS: – *Quick-to-color labels for homemade jams, apple sauce and more.*

BONUS DOWNLOADS FOR PRINTABLE COLOR AND CRAFT PROJECTS
Go to Anni Arts *https://www.anniarts.com/teacher-clip-art.html* for Teacher's Apple freebies.
Get other printable craft freebies from Anni Arts Crafts *https://www.anniartscrafts.com/anni-arts-crafts-freebies.html*

OTHER TEACHER'S APPLE PRODUCTS – Great gifts for teachers, homeschoolers and apple lovers!
– See the coordinating *Teacher's Apple Cut-N-Make Book* with pre-printed paper crafts in red and black chalkboard colors. The items are ready to cut, make and glue for cards, packs and décor.
Anni Arts *https://www.anniarts.com/teachers-apple.html*

– The *Teacher's Apple* designs are also on the printable Anni Arts Paper Crafts and on a craft USB or CD. The printables include Apple Mandala coloring sets too. Anni Arts Crafts *https://www.anniartscrafts.com*

– And ready-to-buy Teacher's Apple products are in the Anni Arts Zazzle Store *www.zazzle.com/store/anniarts*
Or follow links from the Teacher's Apple book page on Anni Arts: *https://www.anniarts.com/teachers-apple.html*

Text, Book Layout, Cover, Illustrations and Crafts by Anneke Lipsanen.
Copyright Anneke Lipsanen. All Rights Reserved. No part of this publication may be reproduced, or transmitted in any form without prior written permission from Anneke Lipsanen. Paperback Edition 2022

EQUIPMENT

Only a few basic items are needed to make these creative apple paper crafts.

PENCIL CRAYONS, MARKERS or COLORED BALL POINT PENS
SCISSORS
CRAFT KNIFE with a sharp blade to cut straight lines (optional)
RULER (With a metal edge if used with a craft knife)
GLUE STICK
ADHESIVE TAPE (Use as an alternative to glue on some items.)
If you use tape, double-sided tape will be preferable as it can be concealed between layers.
PAPER SCORER
The bunting flags, 3D apple decorations and tags have lines to be scored and folded.

A paper scorer is an instrument to draw a line to make folding that line easier.
It makes a dent on the card or paper, but does not cut right through. It is essential for creating tidy and precise paper crafts. Craft shops sell special scoring instruments, but an empty ballpoint pen is just as efficient – and is my personal favorite! You can also use the blunt side of the blade of a craft knife to make a *very light* score. And in a pinch you can also use a butter knife (with no serrations on the blade).
Note: When scoring regular paper like that used in this paper craft book, take care to score lightly – the paper can easily tear if the score runs too deep.

TIPS AND GENERAL INSTRUCTIONS

The pages have relevant instructions printed with the paper craft item.

TIPS

First cut each craft page from the book along the guide line. A craft knife is handy for this.
The pictures for framing are in a ruled box and do not have guide lines
Color before cutting and making the Frame Art, Cards, Bunting, Decorations and Stocking.
(Or first cut a rough shape around the crafts and cards, do the coloring and then tidy the shape by cutting on the outlines.) The apples on the art pages can also be shape-cut when they have been colored and then glued to a patterned base. A red-and-white apple page, cupcake wrappers and envelope is included in the free downloads, as well as extra items to color.
Anni Arts https://www.anniarts.com/teacher-clip-art.html
Score all lines as indicated, fold on the scored lines and glue or assemble as indicated.

GREETING CARDS

Make sure that glue goes all the way to the edges of the card elements. Lay a blank piece of paper over a freshly positioned and glued element and glide the edge of a ruler over the covered section to flatten and properly glue the element to the underlying layer. The cover paper protects the coloring and the glued elements.

The topper patches or shaped cards are glued to blank cards cut from cardstock.
Cut card bases to the dimensions given below, or download the printable blank templates from Anni Arts and print the card bases on printable cardstock at the link below. The card toppers can also be glued to postcards on a single card layer. The cards need purchased envelopes.
Anni Arts https://www.anniarts.com/teacher-clip-art.html

*Cut a **10" x 7"** (approx. 25.5 x 17.75 cm) backing for a card that folds to **5" x 7"** (or cut a 5" x 7" postcard)*
*Cut a **8" x 6"** (approx. 20 x 15 cm) backing for a card that folds to **4" x 6"** (or cut a 4" x 6" postcard)*
Score through the middle to fold the card and add the card making elements to the front.

Get free Teacher's Apple printables at www.anniarts.com/teacher-clip-art.html

Get free Teacher's Apple printables at www.anniarts.com/teacher-clip-art.html

Get free Teacher's Apple printables at www.anniarts.com/teacher-clip-art.html

CARD TOPPERS: Color apples (and background - optional). Cut apple shape or entire rectangular background and glue to cardstock.

Get free Teacher's Apple printables at www.anniarts.com/teacher-clip-art.html

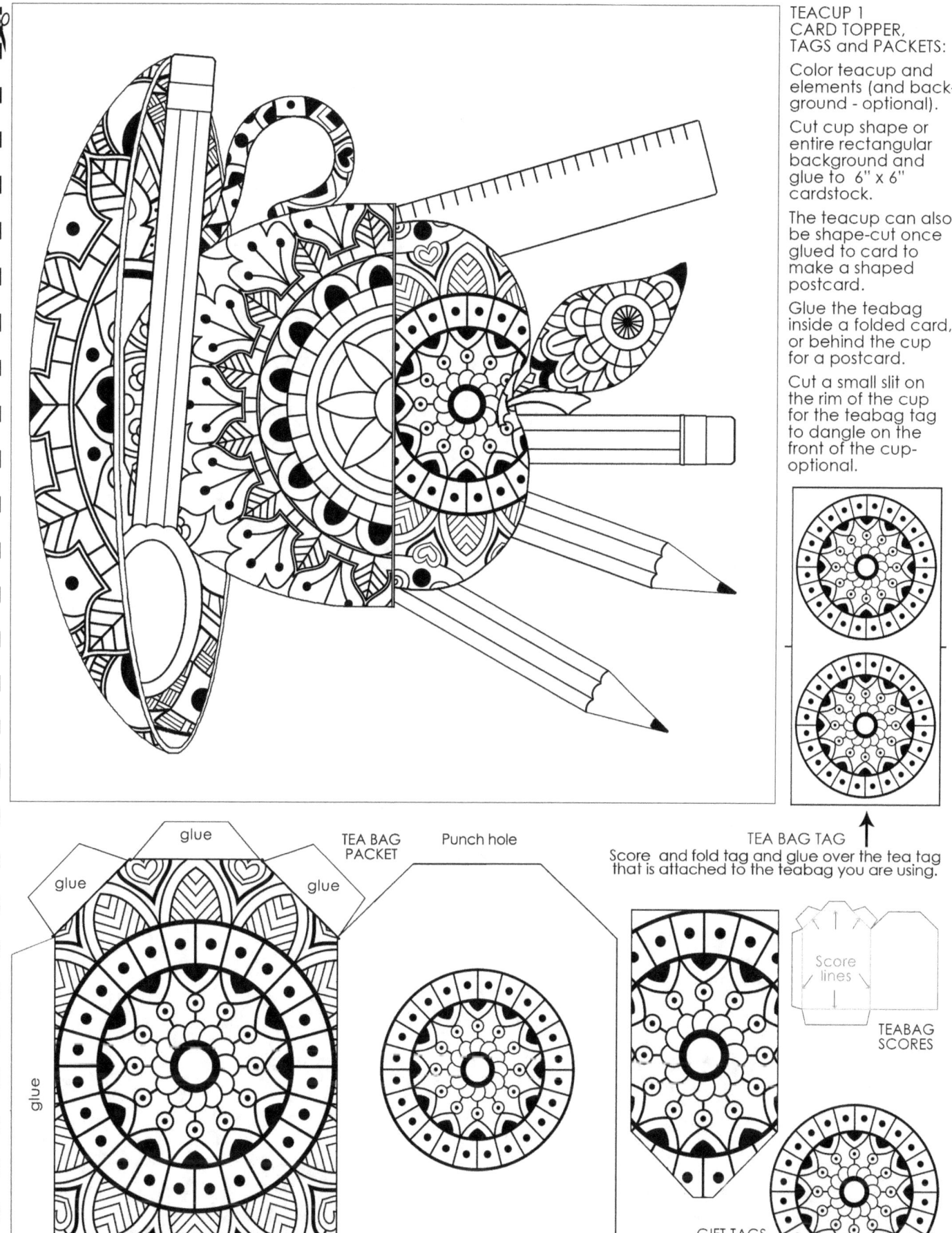

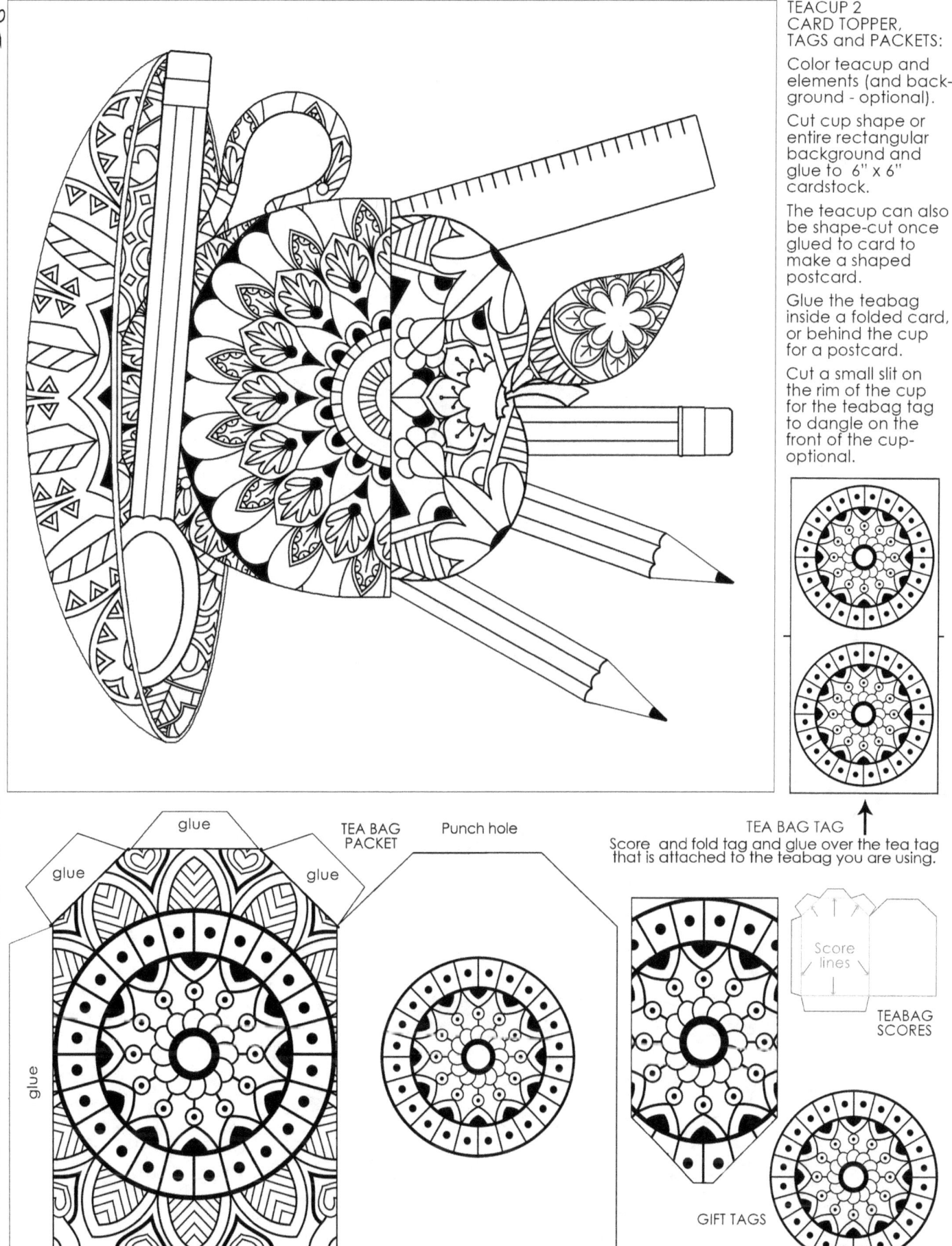

MUG 2 CARD TOPPER, TAGS and PACKETS: Color mug and elements (and background - optional). Cut mug shape or entire rectangular background and glue to 5" x 7" cardstock. The mug can also be shape-cut once glued to card to make a shaped postcard. Glue the teabag inside a folded card, or behind the mug for a postcard. Cut a small slit on the rim of the mug for the teabag tag to dangle on the front of the mug - optional.

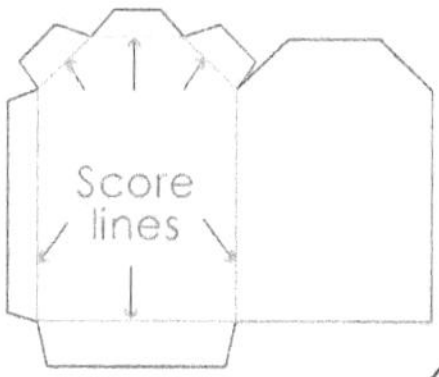

Score lines

TEA BAG TAG
Score and fold tag and glue over the tea tag that is attached to the teabag you are using.

TEABAG SCORES

glue glue glue

TEA BAG PACKET

Punch hole

score

GIFT TAG

GIFT TAG

glue

score glue score

Score light lines and fold. Glue side tab and bottom tab to make packet.
Place teabag in packet, place teabag string through top and glue and close top
TIP: Shake tea leaves in teabag to distribute evenly before placing in packet.

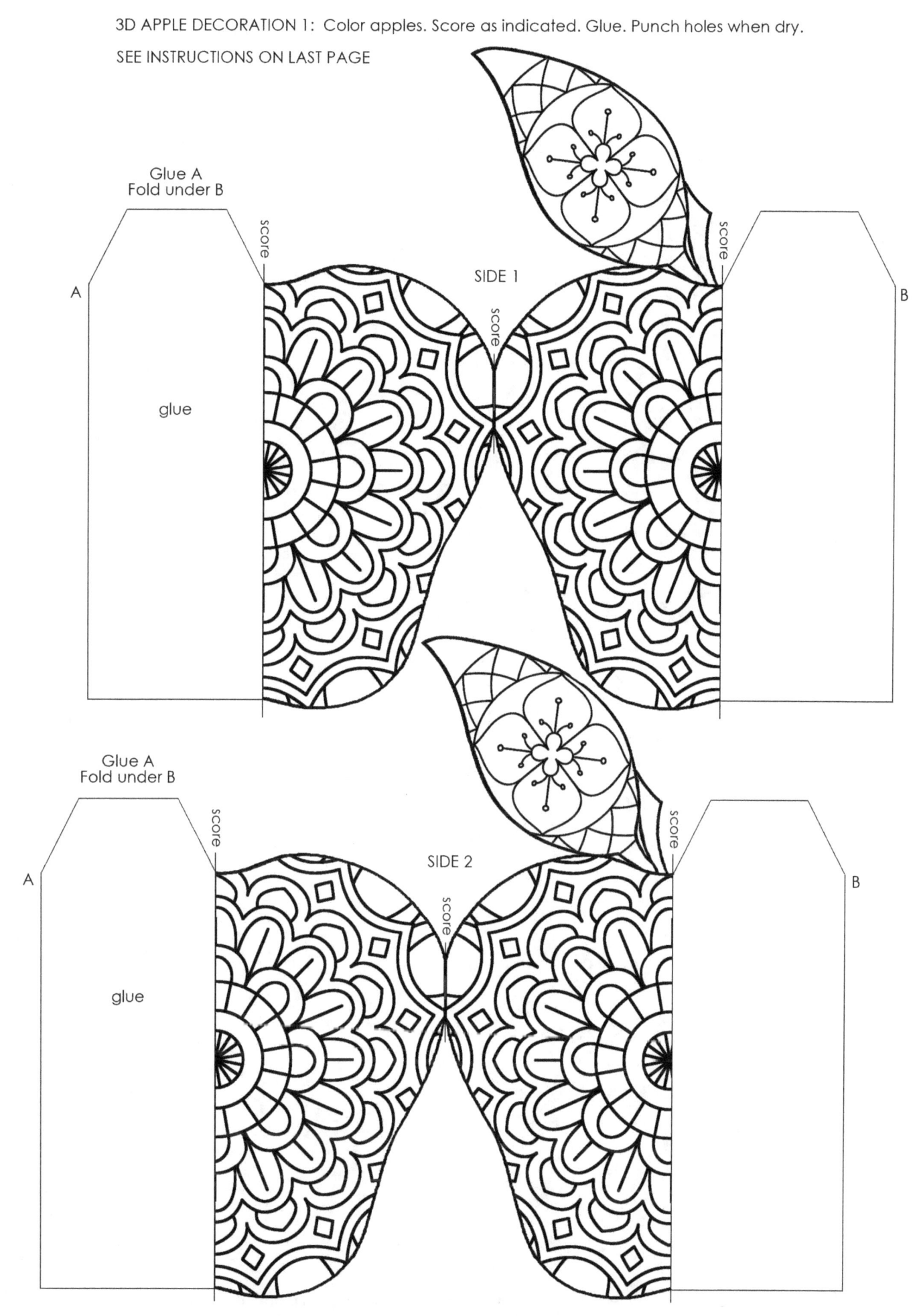

Get free Teacher's Apple printables at www.anniarts.com/teacher-clip-art.html

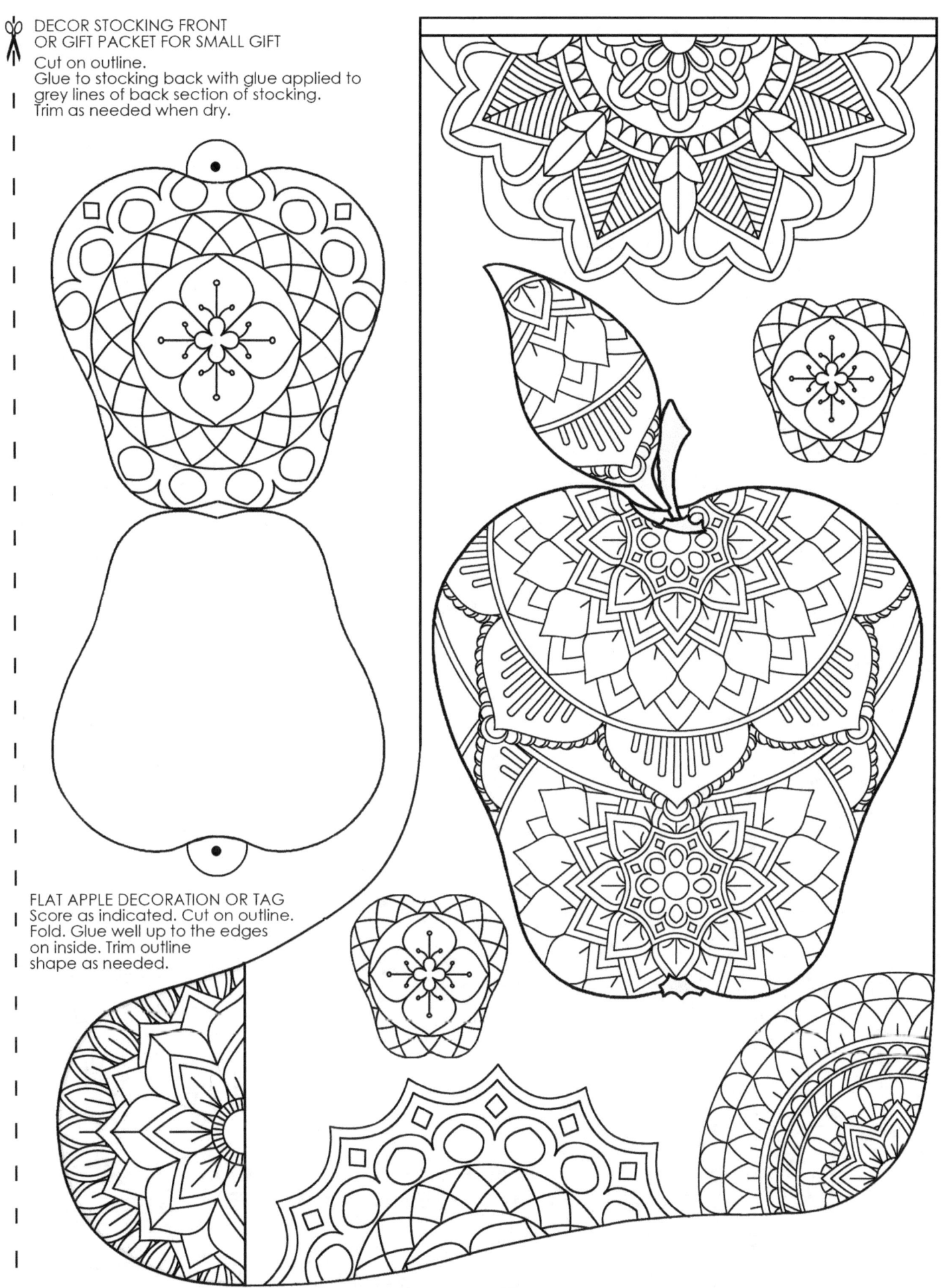

✂ DECOR STOCKING FRONT
OR GIFT PACKET FOR SMALL GIFT
Cut on outline.
Glue to stocking back with glue applied to grey lines of back section of stocking.
Trim as needed when dry.

FLAT APPLE DECORATION OR TAG
Score as indicated. Cut on outline.
Fold. Glue well up to the edges on inside. Trim outline shape as needed.

Get free Teacher's Apple printables at www.anniarts.com/teacher-clip-art.html

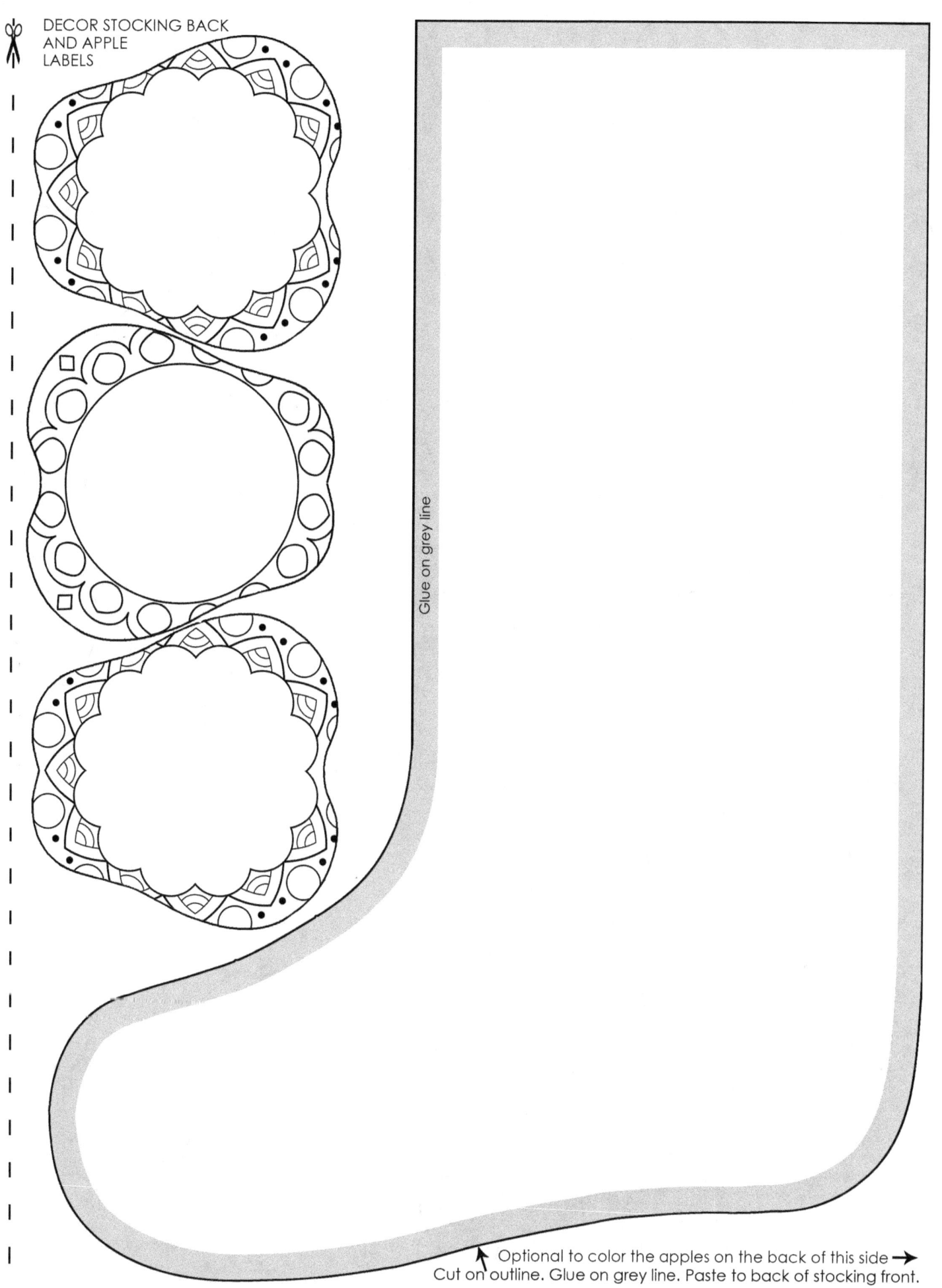

ANNI ARTS
https://www.anniarts.com/

Teacher's Apple book page and links to freebies
https://www.anniarts.com/teachers-apple.html

www.ingramcontent.com/pod-product-compliance
Lightning Source LLC
LaVergne TN
LVHW062001070526
838199LV00060B/4232